EMMANUEL JOSEPH

The Infinite Bridge, Uniting Nations Through Decentralized Market Innovation

Copyright © 2025 by Emmanuel Joseph

All rights reserved. No part of this publication may be reproduced, stored or transmitted in any form or by any means, electronic, mechanical, photocopying, recording, scanning, or otherwise without written permission from the publisher. It is illegal to copy this book, post it to a website, or distribute it by any other means without permission.

First edition

This book was professionally typeset on Reedsy.
Find out more at reedsy.com

Contents

1 Chapter 1: A New Dawn of Global Connectivity   1
2 Chapter 2: The Genesis of Decentralization   3
3 Chapter 3: Building Trust in Decentralized Systems   5
4 Chapter 4: The Role of Technology in Decentralized Markets   7
5 Chapter 5: Empowering Emerging Markets   9
6 Chapter 6: Bridging Cultural Divides   11
7 Chapter 7: Overcoming Regulatory Challenges   13
8 Chapter 8: The Future of Work in Decentralized Markets   15
9 Chapter 9: Environmental Sustainability Through...   17
10 Chapter 10: The Role of Education in Decentralized Markets   19
11 Chapter 11: Social Impact of Decentralized Markets   21
12 Chapter 12: The Road Ahead   23

1

Chapter 1: A New Dawn of Global Connectivity

In recent years, the world has seen an unprecedented surge in technological advancements, fostering a new era of connectivity. This evolution has not only brought individuals closer but has also bridged the gap between nations. The concept of decentralized markets emerges as a beacon of innovation in this landscape, promising to revolutionize global trade and economic collaboration. Decentralization, unlike traditional centralized systems, thrives on transparency, autonomy, and community-driven governance, making it an ideal solution for contemporary global challenges.

At its core, decentralization leverages blockchain technology to create immutable records of transactions, ensuring security and trust among participants. This shift is significant as it eradicates the need for intermediaries, reducing costs and increasing efficiency. Imagine a world where businesses, regardless of their size or geographical location, can engage in trade seamlessly and securely. This vision is no longer a distant dream but a reality that decentralized markets are bringing to life.

However, with great innovation comes great responsibility. As nations navigate this transformative journey, they must address regulatory frameworks, ensure fair participation, and protect against potential abuses. The transition to decentralized markets is not without its hurdles, but the potential benefits far outweigh the challenges. It is a collaborative effort that requires the participation and cooperation of governments, businesses, and individuals alike.

Ultimately, the rise of decentralized markets signifies a new dawn for global connectivity. It heralds a future where economic disparities are minimized, opportunities are democratized, and nations unite through shared prosperity. As we embark on this journey, it is crucial to understand the mechanics of decentralization and harness its power for the greater good.

2

Chapter 2: The Genesis of Decentralization

The concept of decentralization is not entirely new; its roots can be traced back to ancient societies where barter systems facilitated trade. However, the digital revolution has breathed new life into this age-old idea, giving rise to decentralized networks that operate on blockchain technology. The genesis of decentralization lies in the desire to create systems that are more inclusive, transparent, and resistant to corruption.

Blockchain, the backbone of decentralized markets, is a distributed ledger technology that records transactions across multiple computers. This ensures that no single entity has control over the entire network, promoting transparency and trust. The first significant application of blockchain was Bitcoin, a digital currency that introduced the world to the possibilities of decentralized finance. Since then, the technology has evolved, paving the way for a myriad of applications beyond cryptocurrency.

In the context of global trade, decentralized markets offer numerous advantages. They eliminate the need for intermediaries, such as banks and clearinghouses, reducing transaction costs and increasing efficiency. Additionally, they provide a level playing field for all participants, regardless of their size or geographical location. This democratization of trade fosters innovation and competition, driving economic growth and development.

However, the journey towards decentralization is not without its challenges. Issues such as scalability, regulatory compliance, and security must be addressed to ensure the widespread adoption of decentralized markets. Moreover, the transition from traditional systems to decentralized networks requires a paradigm shift in how we perceive and conduct trade. It demands a collective effort from all stakeholders to embrace change and work towards a more inclusive and equitable global economy.

3

Chapter 3: Building Trust in Decentralized Systems

Trust is the cornerstone of any successful economic system, and decentralized markets are no exception. Building trust in these systems requires a combination of technological innovation, regulatory oversight, and community engagement. Blockchain technology plays a pivotal role in this process, as its inherent characteristics of transparency, immutability, and security instill confidence among participants.

One of the primary advantages of blockchain is its ability to create an immutable record of transactions. This feature ensures that once a transaction is recorded, it cannot be altered or tampered with, providing a high level of security and trust. Additionally, the decentralized nature of blockchain means that no single entity has control over the entire network, reducing the risk of fraud and manipulation. These attributes make blockchain an ideal solution for building trust in global trade and economic collaboration.

Regulatory oversight is another crucial aspect of fostering trust in decentralized markets. Governments and regulatory bodies must establish clear guidelines and frameworks to ensure that these systems operate fairly and transparently. This includes addressing issues such as consumer protection, anti-money laundering, and data privacy. By providing a robust regulatory environment, governments can encourage the adoption of decentralized markets while safeguarding the interests of all participants.

Community engagement is equally important in building trust. Decentralized markets thrive on the active participation and collaboration of their users. By involving the community in decision-making processes and governance, these systems can ensure that they remain transparent, accountable, and responsive to the needs of their participants. This collaborative approach not only fosters trust but also promotes a sense of ownership and belonging among users.

4

Chapter 4: The Role of Technology in Decentralized Markets

Technology is the driving force behind the rise of decentralized markets. From blockchain to smart contracts, technological innovations are revolutionizing the way we conduct trade and interact with one another. These advancements not only enhance the efficiency and security of transactions but also create new opportunities for economic collaboration and growth.

Blockchain technology, as previously mentioned, is the backbone of decentralized markets. It provides a secure and transparent platform for recording transactions, ensuring that all participants have access to the same information. This transparency is crucial for building trust and promoting fair competition. Additionally, blockchain enables the creation of smart contracts, which are self-executing agreements with the terms of the contract directly written into code. These contracts automate processes, reduce the risk of errors, and ensure that transactions are carried out efficiently and accurately.

Another technological innovation that plays a significant role in decentralized markets is the Internet of Things (IoT). IoT devices can collect and share data in real-time, providing valuable insights into supply chain management, inventory control, and other aspects of trade. By integrating

IoT with blockchain, businesses can create more efficient and transparent supply chains, reducing costs and improving the overall quality of goods and services.

Artificial intelligence (AI) is also transforming decentralized markets. AI algorithms can analyze vast amounts of data to identify patterns, trends, and potential risks, enabling businesses to make more informed decisions. Moreover, AI can be used to develop predictive models, optimize pricing strategies, and enhance customer experiences. By harnessing the power of AI, businesses can stay competitive and adapt to the ever-changing global market landscape.

5

Chapter 5: Empowering Emerging Markets

Decentralized markets hold tremendous potential for empowering emerging economies. These markets provide an inclusive platform where small and medium-sized enterprises (SMEs) can compete on a global scale. By removing intermediaries and reducing transaction costs, decentralized markets enable businesses in developing nations to access new opportunities and expand their reach.

One of the key benefits of decentralized markets is their ability to provide financial inclusion. In many developing countries, access to traditional banking services is limited, leaving a significant portion of the population unbanked. Decentralized finance (DeFi) platforms offer an alternative by providing financial services through blockchain technology. These platforms enable individuals and businesses to access loans, savings accounts, and other financial products without the need for a traditional bank.

Furthermore, decentralized markets foster innovation and entrepreneurship. They provide a level playing field where new ideas and business models can thrive. By leveraging blockchain technology, entrepreneurs can create transparent and secure ecosystems that attract investors and customers. This, in turn, stimulates economic growth and job creation, contributing to the overall development of emerging markets.

However, the adoption of decentralized markets in emerging economies is not without challenges. Issues such as digital literacy, infrastructure, and regulatory compliance must be addressed to ensure the successful integration of these markets. Governments and international organizations play a crucial role in supporting this transition by providing the necessary resources and creating favorable policies.

6

Chapter 6: Bridging Cultural Divides

One of the most profound impacts of decentralized markets is their ability to bridge cultural divides. By fostering global trade and collaboration, these markets create opportunities for individuals and businesses from diverse backgrounds to interact and learn from one another. This exchange of ideas and perspectives enriches our understanding of different cultures and promotes mutual respect.

Decentralized markets operate on the principles of transparency and inclusivity, which are essential for building trust and fostering collaboration. In traditional markets, cultural barriers and biases can hinder trade and communication. Decentralized markets, on the other hand, provide a neutral platform where participants are judged based on their contributions rather than their cultural background.

Moreover, decentralized markets facilitate cross-border collaborations and partnerships. Businesses can tap into new markets and reach customers from different parts of the world. This not only expands their customer base but also exposes them to different cultural norms and preferences, enabling them to adapt and innovate. For example, a company that understands the cultural nuances of its target market is better equipped to design products and services that meet the needs and preferences of its customers.

The ability to bridge cultural divides also extends to the workforce. Decentralized markets enable businesses to hire talent from different parts of the world, bringing diverse perspectives and skills to the table. This diversity fosters creativity and innovation, leading to the development of new ideas and solutions.

7

Chapter 7: Overcoming Regulatory Challenges

While decentralized markets offer numerous benefits, they also pose regulatory challenges that need to be addressed to ensure their smooth operation. Traditional regulatory frameworks are often ill-equipped to handle the unique characteristics of decentralized markets, necessitating the development of new policies and guidelines.

One of the primary regulatory challenges is ensuring compliance with existing laws and regulations. Decentralized markets operate across borders, making it difficult to enforce regulations that vary from one jurisdiction to another. Governments and regulatory bodies must work together to create harmonized policies that facilitate cross-border trade while ensuring compliance with legal requirements.

Consumer protection is another critical aspect of regulating decentralized markets. As these markets gain popularity, it is essential to establish safeguards that protect consumers from fraud, scams, and other malicious activities. This includes implementing measures such as identity verification, transaction monitoring, and dispute resolution mechanisms. By creating a secure and transparent environment, regulators can build trust among consumers and encourage the adoption of decentralized markets.

Data privacy and security are also significant concerns in decentralized markets. With the increasing amount of data being generated and shared, it is crucial to establish robust data protection policies that safeguard individuals' privacy. This includes implementing measures such as encryption, access controls, and regular audits to ensure that data is handled securely and responsibly.

8

Chapter 8: The Future of Work in Decentralized Markets

The rise of decentralized markets is reshaping the future of work, offering new opportunities and challenges for the global workforce. These markets enable individuals to work remotely, collaborate with diverse teams, and access new income streams, transforming traditional employment models.

One of the key advantages of decentralized markets is their ability to provide flexible work opportunities. Individuals can participate in the gig economy, offering their skills and services to a global audience. This flexibility allows people to work on their terms, balancing their professional and personal lives more effectively. For example, a graphic designer in Nigeria can collaborate with clients in Europe and North America, expanding their reach and earning potential.

Decentralized markets also promote the concept of decentralized autonomous organizations (DAOs). DAOs are community-driven organizations that operate on blockchain technology, allowing members to participate in decision-making and governance. This decentralized approach empowers individuals to have a say in the direction and operations of the organization, fostering a sense of ownership and engagement.

However, the future of work in decentralized markets also presents challenges. Issues such as job security, worker protection, and skill development must be addressed to ensure that the workforce can adapt to the changing landscape. Governments, businesses, and educational institutions must work together to provide the necessary support and resources for individuals to thrive in this new environment.

9

Chapter 9: Environmental Sustainability Through Decentralization

Decentralized markets have the potential to contribute to environmental sustainability by promoting more efficient and transparent supply chains. By leveraging blockchain technology, businesses can track the origin and journey of products, ensuring that they are sourced and produced sustainably.

One of the key benefits of decentralized markets is their ability to reduce waste and inefficiencies. Traditional supply chains often involve multiple intermediaries, leading to delays, excess inventory, and higher carbon emissions. Decentralized markets streamline these processes by eliminating intermediaries and providing real-time visibility into the supply chain. This enables businesses to optimize their operations, reduce waste, and minimize their environmental impact.

Additionally, decentralized markets can promote the use of renewable energy and sustainable practices. Blockchain technology can be used to create transparent and verifiable records of renewable energy production and consumption. This ensures that businesses and consumers can make informed decisions about their energy use and contribute to the transition to a more sustainable energy system.

Furthermore, decentralized markets can support the development of circular economies. By providing a platform for the exchange of goods and services, these markets encourage the reuse and recycling of materials, reducing the need for new resources. For example, a decentralized marketplace for second-hand goods can facilitate the trade of used products, extending their lifecycle and reducing waste.

10

Chapter 10: The Role of Education in Decentralized Markets

Education plays a crucial role in the successful adoption and integration of decentralized markets. As these markets continue to evolve, it is essential to equip individuals with the knowledge and skills they need to navigate this new landscape.

One of the key aspects of education in decentralized markets is raising awareness and understanding of blockchain technology. By incorporating blockchain education into curricula at all levels, from primary schools to universities, we can ensure that the next generation is well-prepared to leverage the opportunities presented by decentralized markets. This includes teaching students about the principles of decentralization, the mechanics of blockchain, and the potential applications of this technology.

In addition to formal education, there is a need for ongoing training and professional development for individuals already in the workforce. As decentralized markets continue to evolve, individuals must stay up-to-date with the latest trends and developments. This can be achieved through workshops, online courses, and industry certifications. By providing access to continuous learning opportunities, we can ensure that individuals have the skills they need to thrive in decentralized markets.

Moreover, education can play a role in fostering innovation and entrepreneurship in decentralized markets. By encouraging a culture of experimentation and risk-taking, educational institutions can nurture the next generation of innovators and entrepreneurs. This includes providing access to resources such as incubators, accelerators, and mentorship programs that support the development of new ideas and business models.

11

Chapter 11: Social Impact of Decentralized Markets

Decentralized markets have the potential to create significant social impact by promoting inclusivity, equity, and empowerment. These markets provide a platform for individuals and communities that have been traditionally marginalized to participate in the global economy and benefit from new opportunities.

One of the key social impacts of decentralized markets is their ability to promote financial inclusion. By providing access to financial services through blockchain technology, these markets enable individuals in underserved communities to save, invest, and build wealth. This can help reduce poverty and improve the overall quality of life for millions of people around the world.

Decentralized markets also promote gender equity by providing equal opportunities for women to participate in the economy. In many parts of the world, women face barriers to accessing financial services, starting businesses, and engaging in trade. Decentralized markets can help break down these barriers by providing a level playing field where everyone, regardless of gender, has an equal chance to succeed.

Furthermore, decentralized markets can empower local communities by enabling them to create their own economic ecosystems. By leveraging blockchain technology, communities can develop localized markets that support local businesses and promote sustainable development. This can help build resilient and self-sufficient communities that are less dependent on external resources and more capable of addressing their own needs.

12

Chapter 12: The Road Ahead

Includes embracing decentralized autonomous organizations (DAOs), investing in blockchain infrastructure, and promoting digital literacy among employees and stakeholders. By fostering a culture of innovation and adaptability, businesses can stay competitive and contribute to the growth of decentralized markets.

Individuals also have a vital role to play in the success of decentralized markets. By educating themselves about blockchain technology and decentralized finance, individuals can take advantage of new opportunities for investment, entrepreneurship, and collaboration. This requires a proactive approach to learning and staying informed about the latest trends and developments in the field.

Furthermore, collaboration and partnerships are essential for the growth and sustainability of decentralized markets. Governments, businesses, and individuals must work together to create an ecosystem that supports innovation, inclusivity, and transparency. This includes sharing best practices, developing open-source technologies, and fostering a sense of community and trust among participants.

As we move forward, it is crucial to remain mindful of the potential challenges and risks associated with decentralized markets. Issues such as scalability, security, and regulatory compliance must be addressed to ensure the long-term success and stability of these markets. By taking a proactive and collaborative approach, we can overcome these challenges and unlock the full potential of decentralized markets for the benefit of all.

The journey towards a decentralized future is an exciting and transformative one. It promises to reshape the global economy, create new opportunities for innovation and growth, and bring nations closer together through shared prosperity. As we continue to explore and embrace the possibilities of decentralized markets, we must remain committed to the principles of transparency, inclusivity, and sustainability. Together, we can build a brighter and more connected future for all.

Book Description: The Infinite Bridge: Uniting Nations Through Decentralized Market Innovation

In an era of rapid technological advancements, "The Infinite Bridge" explores the transformative power of decentralized markets to unite nations and create a more inclusive and equitable global economy. This compelling book delves into the principles of decentralization, the innovative potential of blockchain technology, and the profound impact of decentralized markets on global trade, financial inclusion, and social equity.

Through a series of insightful chapters, readers will discover how decentralized markets eliminate intermediaries, reduce transaction costs, and provide a level playing field for businesses of all sizes. The book highlights the role of technology, from blockchain to artificial intelligence, in revolutionizing supply chains, promoting sustainability, and empowering emerging economies.

"The Infinite Bridge" also examines the regulatory challenges and opportunities associated with decentralized markets, emphasizing the importance of robust frameworks and international collaboration. It explores the social impact of these markets, showcasing their potential to promote gender equity, financial inclusion, and community empowerment.

With a forward-looking perspective, "The Infinite Bridge" envisions a future where decentralized markets foster innovation, bridge cultural divides, and create a more connected and prosperous world. This book is a must-read for anyone interested in the intersection of technology, economics, and global development.

www.ingramcontent.com/pod-product-compliance
Lightning Source LLC
LaVergne TN
LVHW020744090526
838202LV00057BA/6222